BEYONCÉ LEGENDS ALPHABET

Words by Robin Feiner

Aa

A is for All Night.
Yoncé has never shied
away from honesty. On
this horns and strings-filled
ballad from Lemonade,
she's finally ready to forgive
Jay-Z, fall back in love, and
into his arms. 'Found the
truth beneath your lies,
and true love never has
to hide!'

B is for **B**aby Boy.
With foot-stomping rhythm and a smooth Sean Paul verse, it's no surprise this single topped the charts. Beyoncé is over the moon about her 'Baby Boy,' and can't get him out of her fantasies. 'I think about you all the time, I see you in my dreams!'

C is for Crazy in Love. The first single from the Dangerously in Love album boldly announced Queen Bey's solo career to the world. Heavy on the horns and with a killer cameo from Jay-Z, this crazy popular hit is all about how love can make you feel crazy!

D is for **Dr**unk in Love. Full of attitude and power, this hit off her self-titled album puts her passion on full display. Alongside her hubby Jay-Z, this is Bey at her boldest. No wonder the tune was paid respect by Rolling Stone magazine and the Grammys.

E is for Ego.
Fun, flirty, and upbeat,
on Ego Beyoncé tells how
enchanting swagger can
be. As she once told The
London Times, she loves
a man who's strong and
confident, just like her boo,
Jay-Z. 'He got a big ego...
such a huge ego... I love
his big ego!'

Ff

F is for **F**ormation.
'I got hot sauce in my bag, swag.' On this 3x platinum hit, Yoncé is packing more style and confidence than ever. She's proud of her Texas-Bama roots, proud to be Black, and of being a country girl, too. Now, it's time for all her ladies to fall in formation!

Gg

G is for Run the World (Girls). Mixing African, futuristic and electronic sounds, this club hit has a special place in Bey's heart. It's a strong message to all the queens out there, reminding them of who's really in charge. 'Who run the world? Girls!'

H is for Halo.
Heavenly and glorious,
on this ballad from I Am...
Sasha Fierce, Queen Bey
bares her romantic side.
She's met a man she can
trust, and their love is
so strong that it's like a
guardian angel is watching
over her. 'Baby I can feel
your halo, pray it won't
fade away!'

I is for Irreplaceable.
This Queen Bey classic was
2007's biggest song! Over
a catchy acoustic melody,
she warns her man that he
can be easily replaced if he
ever betrays her. 'I can have
another you in a minute,
matter fact he'll be here in
a minute!'

J is for **J**ealous.
On this power ballad,
Beyoncé is not happy with
her man. He stood her up
for dinner and made her feel
jealous, but that doesn't
mean she won't get the last
laugh. 'I'm staying out till
tomorrow, dancing on them
tables, ain't got no cares,
no sorrow!'

K is for **K**itty Kat.
On this slower jam from her second album, Queen Bey's feeling neglected. Her man's keeping her waiting. But hey, it's his loss. She's powerful and independent... so she packs up her things. 'Let's go, let's go, let's go, little kitty cat.'

L is for Daddy **L**essons.
'He told me not to cry, oh, my daddy said shoot.'
In 2016, Yoncé returned to her Houston roots with this catchy country classic. It's all about how her daddy raised her, how he taught her to be strong, confident, and stand up for herself. Isn't that exactly what dads are for?

M is for **M**e, Myself & I. Who do you turn to when there's no one to trust? Bey answered that with this slow, personal tune with a feminist theme. A reminder that if a girl can't trust a man, she can always trust herself. 'Me, myself and I, that's all I got in the end.'

N is for Say My **N**ame. Before going solo, Bey belted her soul out alongside the other members of Destiny's Child. This group from Houston could sing and dance like there was no tomorrow. 'You acting kinda shady, ain't calling me baby, why the sudden change?'

Oo

O is for Love **O**n Top. This '80s-style, Grammy-winning R&B tune was inspired by the likes of Stevie Wonder and the Jacksons. Queen Bey's got her eyes locked on the ultimate man, a lover who can do no wrong. 'You're the one I love! You're the one I need! You're the only one I see!'

P is for **P**artition.
Back in '13, Yoncé shocked
her BeyHive with a surprise
self-titled album. This pop-
rap hit from that album is
all about getting privacy
when you need it most.
But it's so hard to take
your eyes off Bey, right?

Q is for **Q**ueen Bey.
JuJu, Bey, Sasha Fierce—
no matter what you call her,
she's the Queen. She's won
a record 32 Grammys, has
the world's most loyal
BeyHive, and sings proudly
about body positivity and
Black rights. Yoncé is simply
the greatest R&B star ever.

R is for **R**ing the Alarm. 'How can you look at me and not see all the things that I kept only just for you?' On this passionate track, Yoncé doesn't want to see her ex happy with some other woman. After all, she taught him everything he knows.

S is for Single Ladies (Put a Ring on It). 'If you liked it then you shoulda put a ring on it!' This classic reminds girls everywhere of one simple thing: If he takes too long to propose, dump him! With three Grammy wins, it's one of Queen Bey's best.

T is for Telephone.
What happens when the world's biggest popstars combine forces? They come up with a 5x-platinum hit about female independence. On this hit, all Beyoncé and Gaga want is for their ex to stop calling so they can dance the night away in the club!

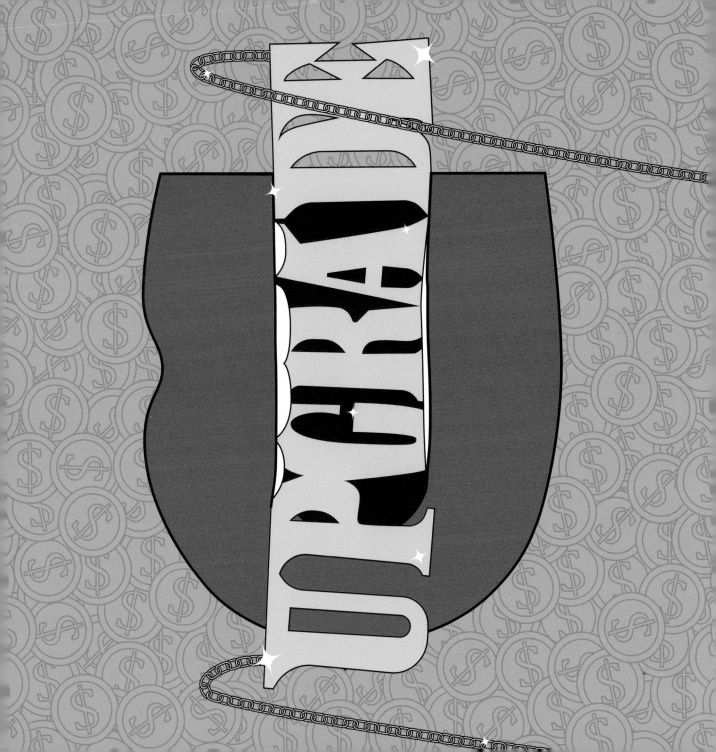

U is for Upgrade U.
In this flashy hip-hop tune,
Queen Bey is showing
Jay-Z all the ways she
can make him better.
'Big ends, condos, collecting
cars—picture your life
elevatin' with me.' When
she's through with him,
he'll be a brand-new man!

V is for Déjà **V**u.
On this hit from 2006, JuJu and Jay-Z are caught in a loop. They can't get over each other, can't stop seeing each other, and can't stop kissing each other. Their love is like constant déjà vu. 'Baby, seem like everywhere I go, I see you.'

Ww

W is for If I **W**ere a Boy. Here, Bey looks at the world through a man's eyes and sings about all the ways men can be better husbands, fathers, and friends. With a soaring melody, this is one of the most powerful songs she's ever created.

X is for **XO.**
'Before they turn the lights out, baby love me lights out!' Queen Bey sings of a love so strong it can light up the blackest of rooms. She can see him in the 'darkest night hour,' and she's ready to give him everything she has.

Y is for Don't Hurt Yourself. Pop, rap, country, blues— Bey can do it all. On this hit, she showed she can even be a rock 'n' roll queen. Alongside Jack White, she tells her bae to try harder, love her more deeply, and not hurt himself in the process. 'Uh, this is your final warning!'

Z is for Jay-**Z**.
Hova, H-to-the-O-V, Shawn
Carter: He's a rap god and
our R&B Queen's hubby.
They met in Cancun, fell
in love, and had a secret
marriage in '08. With their
kids Blue Ivy, Rumi, and Sir
Carter by their sides, Jay
and Bey are the ultimate
power family.

The ever-expanding legendary library

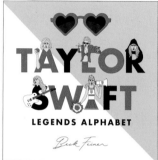

EXPLORE THESE LEGENDARY ALPHABETS & MORE AT WWW.ALPHABETLEGENDS.COM

BEYONCÉ LEGENDS ALPHABET
www.alphabetlegends.com

Published by Alphabet Legends Pty Ltd in 2023
Created by Beck Feiner
Copyright © Alphabet Legends Pty Ltd 2023

Printed and bound in China.

9780645851557